Return to an Address of the Honourable the House of Commons dated 15 June 2010

Principal Conclusions and Overall Assessment of the
Bloody Sunday Inquiry

The Rt Hon The Lord Saville of Newdigate (Chairman)
The Hon William Hoyt OC
The Hon John Toohey AC

Ordered by the House of Commons to be printed on 15 June 2010

The Principal Conclusions and Overall Assessment
(Chapters 1–5 of the report) are reproduced in this volume

This volume is accompanied by a DVD containing the full text of the Report
of the Bloody Sunday Inquiry (HC29), as ordered by the House of Commons
to be printed on 15 June 2010

HC30   London: The Stationery Office   £19.50

200853168

ISBN: 9780102964691

Printed in the UK for The Stationery Office Limited
on behalf of the Controller of Her Majesty's Stationery Office

ID 2355189 06/10

Printed on paper containing 75% recycled fibre content minimum

Principal Conclusions and Overall Assessment of the **Bloody Sunday Inquiry**

The Rt Hon The Lord Saville of Newdigate (Chairman)
The Hon William Hoyt OC
The Hon John Toohey AC

Principal Conclusions and Overall Assessment

Contents

Chapter 1: Introduction

1.1   The object of the Inquiry was to examine the circumstances that led to loss of life in connection with the civil rights march in Londonderry on 30th January 1972. Thirteen civilians were killed by Army gunfire on the day. The day has become generally known as Bloody Sunday, which is why at the outset we called this Inquiry the Bloody Sunday Inquiry. In 1972 Lord Widgery, then the Lord Chief Justice of England, held an inquiry into these same events.

1.2   In these opening chapters of the report we provide an outline of events before and during 30th January 1972; and collect together for convenience the principal conclusions that we have reached on the events of that day. We also provide our overall assessment of what happened on Bloody Sunday. This outline, our principal conclusions and our overall assessment are based on a detailed examination and evaluation of the evidence, which can be found elsewhere in this report. These chapters should be read in conjunction with that detailed examination and evaluation, since there are many important details, including our reasons for the conclusions that we have reached, which we do not include here, in order to avoid undue repetition.

1.3   The Inquiry involved an examination of a complex set of events. In relation to the day itself, most of these events were fast moving and many occurred more or less simultaneously. In order to carry out a thorough investigation into events that have given rise to great controversy over many years, our examination necessarily involved the close consideration and analysis of a very large amount of evidence.

1.4   In addition to those killed, people were also injured by Army gunfire on Bloody Sunday. We took the view at the outset that it would be artificial in the extreme to ignore the injured, since those shooting incidents in the main took place in the same circumstances, at the same times and in the same places as those causing fatal injuries.

1.5   We found it necessary not to confine our investigations only to what happened on the day. Without examining what led up to Bloody Sunday, it would be impossible to reach a properly informed view of what happened, let alone of why it happened. An examination of what preceded Bloody Sunday was particularly important because there had been allegations that members of the United Kingdom and Northern Ireland Governments, as well as the security forces, had so conducted themselves in the period up to Bloody Sunday that they bore a heavy responsibility for what happened on that day.

1.6　　Many of the soldiers (including all those whose shots killed and injured people on Bloody Sunday) were granted anonymity at the Inquiry, after rulings by the Court of Appeal in London. We also granted other individuals anonymity, on the basis of the principles laid down by the Court of Appeal. Those granted anonymity were given ciphers in place of their names. We have preserved their anonymity in this report.

1.7　　Londonderry is the second largest city in Northern Ireland. It lies in the north-west, close to the border with the country of Ireland. The River Foyle flows through the city. The area of the city with which this report is principally concerned lies on the western side of this river, as does the old walled part of the city. We show the western part of the city and certain important features as they were in 1972 in the following photograph and map.

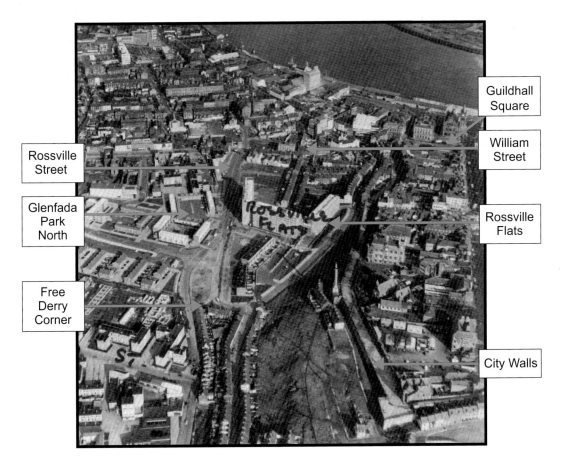

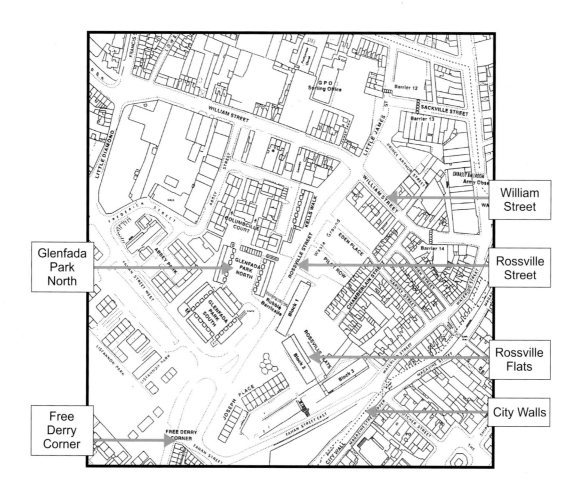

Chapter 2: Outline of events before the day

2.1   Londonderry in January 1972 was a troubled city with a divided society, in a troubled and divided country. Throughout much of Northern Ireland there were deep and seemingly irreconcilable divisions between nationalists (predominantly Roman Catholic and a majority in the city) and unionists (generally Protestant and a majority in Northern Ireland as a whole). In general terms the former wanted Northern Ireland to leave the United Kingdom and unite with the rest of Ireland, while the latter wanted it to remain part of the United Kingdom.

2.2   This sectarian divide, as it was called, had existed for a long time. Among other things, it had led in the years preceding Bloody Sunday to many violent clashes between the two communities and with the police, then the Royal Ulster Constabulary (RUC). The police had become regarded by many in the nationalist community not as impartial keepers of the peace and upholders of the law, but rather as agents of the unionist Northern Ireland Government, employed in their view to keep the nationalist community subjugated, often by the use of unjustifiable and brutal force.

2.3   On 14th August 1969, after there had been particularly violent clashes between civilians and the police in Londonderry, the authorities brought into the city units of the British Army as an aid to the civil power, in other words to restore law and order. The British Army was in the city in this role on Bloody Sunday.

2.4   There was a further dimension in the form of paramilitary organisations. By the beginning of the 1970s the Irish Republican Army (IRA) had split into two organisations known respectively as the Provisional IRA and the Official IRA. These paramilitary organisations (often referred to simply as the IRA, though they were distinct organisations) had restarted a campaign of armed violence, in the belief that only by such means could Northern Ireland be freed from what they regarded as the yoke of British colonial domination and become part of a united Ireland. There were also those on the unionist side of the sectarian divide who organised and used armed violence in the belief that this was required to maintain the union with the United Kingdom.

2.5   This further dimension meant that the security forces, in addition to their other responsibilities, had to deal with those using armed violence.

2.6   The situation in Londonderry in January 1972 was serious. By this stage the nationalist
         community had largely turned against the soldiers, many believing that the Army, as well
         as the RUC, were agents of an oppressive regime. Parts of the city to the west of the
         Foyle lay in ruins, as the result of the activities of the IRA and of rioting young men (some
         members of the IRA or its junior wing, the Fianna) known to soldiers and some others as
         the "Derry Young Hooligans". A large part of the nationalist area of the city was a "no go"
         area, which was dominated by the IRA, where ordinary policing could not be conducted
         and where even the Army ventured only by using large numbers of soldiers.

2.7   The armed violence had led to many casualties. There had been numerous clashes
         between the security forces and the IRA in which firearms had been used on both sides
         and in which the IRA had thrown nail and petrol bombs. Over the months and years
         before Bloody Sunday civilians, soldiers, policemen and IRA gunmen and bombers had
         been killed and wounded; and at least in Londonderry, in January 1972 the violence
         showed few signs of abating.

2.8   In August 1971 the Northern Ireland Government (with the agreement of the United
         Kingdom Government) had introduced internment without trial of suspected terrorists; and
         at the same time had imposed a ban on marches and processions, giving as the reason
         that the former would assist in dealing with armed violence and that the latter would
         reduce the opportunity for violent confrontations between nationalists and unionists.

2.9   The nationalist community in particular regarded internment without trial with abhorrence,
         considering it yet another illegitimate means employed by the unionist Government. Both
         nationalists and unionists expressed opposition to the ban on marches and processions.

2.10   Many people were interned without trial, almost without exception Catholics from the
         nationalist community. Over the following months there were allegations that those held
         had been mistreated, allegations that in significant respects were eventually found to
         have substance.

2.11   By January 1972 the Northern Ireland Civil Rights Association had decided to defy the
         ban on marches. In particular they organised a march in Londonderry to protest against
         internment without trial. This was the march that took place on Bloody Sunday.

2.12   The authorities knew of the proposed march and that the organisers had planned a route
         to Guildhall Square (also known as Shipquay Place), outside the city Guildhall, where
         prominent people would address the marchers. The authorities took the view that the
         security forces should prevent the march from proceeding as planned, fearing that this

flouting of the ban would undermine law and order and would be likely to lead to a violent reaction from unionists. This view prevailed, notwithstanding a contrary view expressed by Chief Superintendent Frank Lagan, the senior police officer in charge of the Londonderry area, who advised that the march should be allowed to proceed. The march was expected to be too large for the police to be able to control it themselves, so the Army shouldered the main burden of dealing with it. The plan that emerged was to allow the march to proceed in the nationalist areas of the city, but to stop it from reaching Guildhall Square by erecting barriers on the roads leading to Guildhall Square, manned by soldiers who were stationed in the area. In the circumstances that obtained at the time, and despite the view expressed by Chief Superintendent Lagan, it was not unreasonable of the authorities to seek to deal with the march in this way.

2.13 At the beginning of January 1972, Major General Robert Ford, then Commander of Land Forces in Northern Ireland, had visited Londonderry. He wrote a confidential memorandum to Lieutenant General Sir Harry Tuzo, his senior and the General Officer Commanding Northern Ireland, in which he expressed himself disturbed by the attitude of the officers commanding the resident troops and that of Chief Superintendent Lagan. He recorded that they had told him that the area of damage in the city was extending and that even the major shopping centre would be destroyed in the coming months. He referred in particular to the "Derry Young Hooligans" as a factor in the continued destruction of the city, and expressed the view that the Army was *"virtually incapable"* of dealing with them. He also expressed the view that he was coming to the conclusion that the minimum force required to deal with the "Derry Young Hooligans" was, after clear warnings, to shoot selected ringleaders.

2.14 The suggestion that selected ringleaders should be shot was not put forward as a means of dealing with the forthcoming civil rights march or any rioting that might accompany it.

2.15 As part of the plan for dealing with the march, what General Ford did do was to order that an additional Army battalion be sent to the city to be used to arrest rioters if, which was expected to happen, the march was followed by rioting. Initially he expressed the view that such a force might be able to arrest a large number of rioters and by that means significantly decrease the activities of the "Derry Young Hooligans".

2.16 To that end General Ford ordered that 1st Battalion, The Parachute Regiment (1 PARA), which was stationed near Belfast, should travel to Londonderry and be used as the arrest force.

2.17   The detailed plan for controlling the march was the responsibility of Brigadier Patrick MacLellan, the Commander of 8th Infantry Brigade, which was the Army brigade in charge of the Londonderry area. The Operation Order (for what was called Operation Forecast) set out the plan that Brigadier MacLellan and his staff had prepared. The Operation Order provided for the use of 1 PARA as the arrest force, but also made clear in express terms that any arrest operation was to be mounted only on the orders of the Brigadier.

Chapter 3: The events of the day

Contents

Events before the arrest operation

3.1   1 PARA arrived in Londonderry on the morning of Sunday 30th January 1972. During the morning and early afternoon Lieutenant Colonel Derek Wilford, the Commanding Officer of 1 PARA, organised the disposition of his soldiers in the city. In addition, the soldiers stationed in the area erected barricades on the streets leading to Guildhall Square and manned those barriers.

3.2   We set out below a map showing some significant buildings, the position of the three most important of the barriers and the numbers that were given to them.

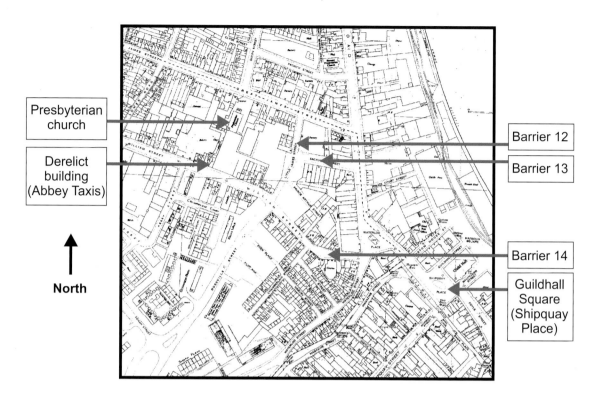

Presbyterian church

Derelict building (Abbey Taxis)

Barrier 12

Barrier 13

Barrier 14

Guildhall Square (Shipquay Place)

North

3.3   Colonel Wilford placed Support Company, one of the companies of 1 PARA, near the Presbyterian church in Great James Street. His initial plan was to send soldiers from there directly south into William Street if rioting broke out in the area and Brigadier MacLellan ordered an arrest operation. However, Colonel Wilford then realised that there were walls that made it difficult for soldiers to move at any speed from Great James Street into William Street, so in order to reduce this drawback he ordered the Commander of Support Company (Major Edward Loden) to be ready to locate one of his platoons in a derelict building (often called "Abbey Taxis" after a taxi firm that once operated from there) on the William Street side of the Presbyterian church. Major Loden selected Machine Gun Platoon for this task and sent this platoon forward. We show below a photograph in which we have identified William Street, the Presbyterian church and the derelict building.

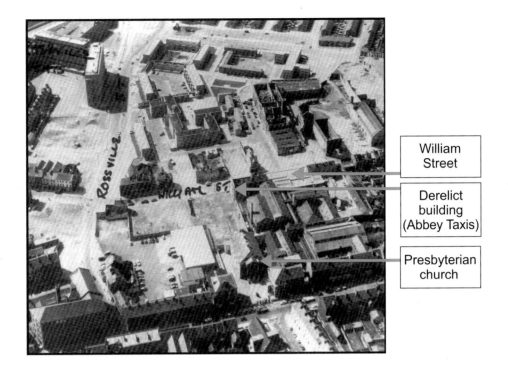

3.4   Meanwhile the civil rights march, many thousands strong, had started in the Creggan area of the city and made its way by a circuitous route through the nationalist part of the city and into William Street. The organisers had planned for and advertised the march to go to Guildhall Square, but at the last moment, knowing that the security forces were going to prevent the march from reaching this destination, they decided instead on a different route; so that when the march reached the junction of William Street and Rossville Street, it would turn right and go along Rossville Street to Free Derry Corner in the Bogside, where there would be speeches. We set out below a map that indicates the original and changed routes of the march and a photograph showing the march proceeding down William Street.

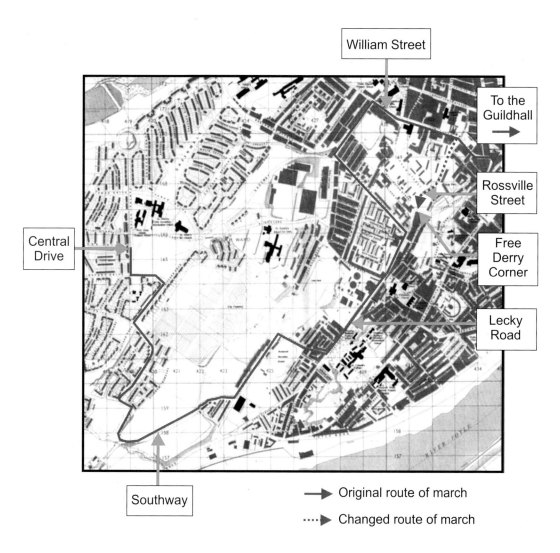

William Street

To the Guildhall →

Rossville Street

Free Derry Corner

Central Drive

Lecky Road

Southway

→ Original route of march

····▶ Changed route of march

3.5   When the march reached the junction of William Street, and Rossville Street, many people, including those who were eager for a confrontation with the security forces, instead of turning right into Rossville Street to go to Free Derry Corner, continued along William Street to the Army barrier there, Barrier 14.

3.6   Shortly after the arrival of people at Barrier 14, rioting broke out there, in the form of members of the crowd throwing stones and similar missiles at the soldiers. In addition, further back, similar rioting broke out at the barriers closing Little James Street and Sackville Street, Barriers 12 and 13. As can be seen from the map shown at paragraph 3.2 above, Little James Street led north from the junction of William Street and Rossville Street, a junction known to soldiers and some others at the time as "Aggro Corner", because it had frequently been an area for riots. Sackville Street led east from Little James Street. There was also rioting of a similar kind further west along William Street, in the area where Machine Gun Platoon was located.

3.7   The soldiers at the barriers responded to the rioting by firing baton rounds (often called rubber bullets) and at Barrier 12 (and perhaps Barrier 13) by firing CS gas. At Barrier 14, rioters themselves threw a canister of CS gas at the soldiers, while the soldiers there, in addition to firing baton rounds, deployed a water cannon and sprayed the rioters (and others who were there) in an attempt to disperse them. The soldiers at Barrier 14 (who were from 2nd Battalion, The Royal Green Jackets) acted with restraint in the face of the rioting at this barrier and deployed no more than properly proportionate force in seeking to deal with it.

3.8   While this rioting was taking place and at just after 1555 hours, Colonel Wilford, who had taken up a position close to the Presbyterian church, sent a radio message to Brigade Headquarters (stationed at Ebrington Barracks on the other side of the River Foyle) in which he suggested sending one of his companies through Barrier 14 (the barrier on William Street) into the area of William Street and Little James Street (ie the area of and to the north of Aggro Corner) on the grounds that by doing so he might be able to arrest a number of rioters. We set out below a map on which we show this area.

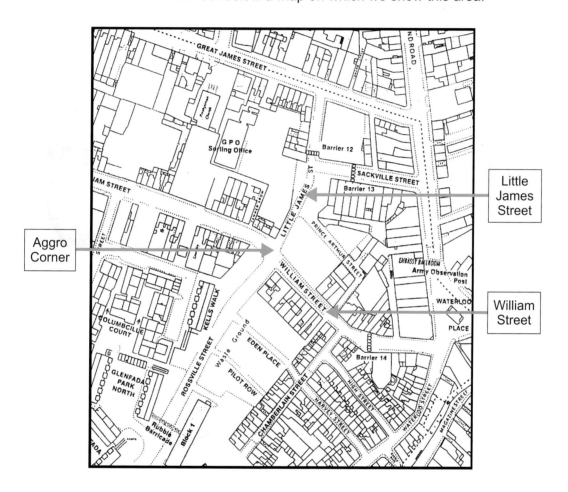

3.9   Brigadier MacLellan, who was at Brigade Headquarters, did not give an order for an arrest operation until some minutes later.

3.10   At about the same time as Colonel Wilford sent this message, two soldiers of Machine Gun Platoon fired between them five shots from the derelict building on William Street, shown on the map below. Their target was Damien Donaghey (aged 15), who was on the other side of William Street and who was wounded in the thigh. Unknown to the soldiers John Johnston (aged 55), who was a little distance behind Damien Donaghey, was also hit and injured by fragments from this gunfire.

3.11   Shortly after this incident a member of the Official IRA (given the cipher OIRA 1) fired a rifle at soldiers who were on a wall on the side of the Presbyterian church. The shot was fired from a position across William Street. We set out below a map showing the area in which these casualties occurred and the position from which OIRA 1 fired.

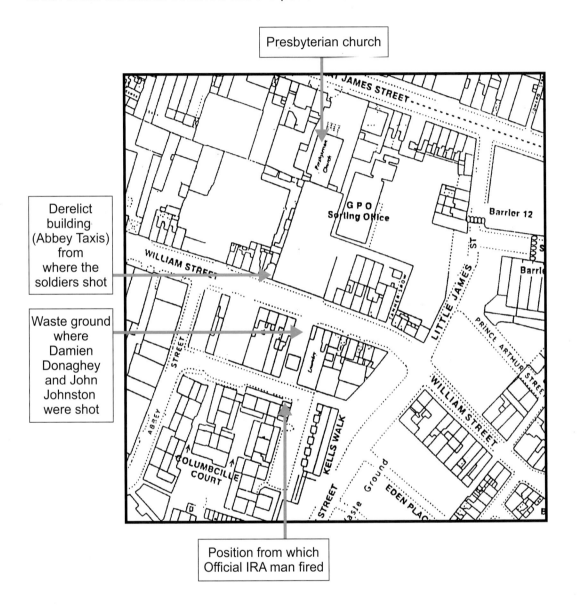

3.12   The shot fired by OIRA 1 missed soldiers and hit a drainpipe running down the side of the Presbyterian church. OIRA 1 and another Official IRA man with him (OIRA 2) insisted that this shot had been fired as a reprisal for the shooting of Damien Donaghey and John Johnston. We were not convinced of this, although we considered on balance that the IRA shot was fired after the wounding of Damien Donaghey and John Johnston. In our view these two Official IRA members had gone to a pre-arranged sniping position in order to fire at the soldiers; and probably did so when an opportunity presented itself rather than because two civilians had been injured.

3.13   At around the time of these incidents Colonel Wilford abandoned his initial plan to send Support Company soldiers from Great James Street directly south into William Street if he got the order to mount an arrest operation; and instead told Support Company to be prepared to go in vehicles through Barrier 12, the barrier in Little James Street.

The arrest operation

3.14   At 1607 hours Brigadier MacLellan gave 1 PARA orders by radio to mount an arrest operation by sending one company of 1 PARA through Barrier 14 in William Street, but not to conduct a running battle down Rossville Street. In its context, the prohibition on conducting a running battle down Rossville Street meant that the soldiers were not to chase people down that street.

3.15   Brigadier MacLellan had delayed giving an order for an arrest operation because he was correctly concerned that there should be separation between rioters and peaceful marchers before launching an operation to arrest the former. He gave the order when he had reasonable grounds for believing that there was such separation in the area for arrests that Colonel Wilford had previously identified.

3.16   This order was responsive to the request made by Colonel Wilford some 12 minutes earlier. In other words, Brigadier MacLellan authorised the arrest operation suggested by Colonel Wilford. The second part of this order reflected Brigadier MacLellan's anxiety that the soldiers should not become mixed up with the peaceful marchers further along Rossville Street.

3.17   The arrest operation ordered by the Brigadier was accordingly limited to sending one company through Barrier 14 in William Street, in an attempt to arrest rioters in the area of and to the north of Aggro Corner.

3.18   Colonel Wilford did not comply with Brigadier MacLellan's order. He deployed one company through Barrier 14 as he was authorised to do, but in addition and without authority he deployed Support Company in vehicles through Barrier 12 in Little James Street. As we describe below, the vehicles travelled along Rossville Street and into the Bogside, where the soldiers disembarked. The effect was that soldiers of Support Company did chase people down Rossville Street. Some of those people had been rioting but many were peaceful marchers. There was thus no separation between peaceful marchers and those who had been rioting and no means whereby soldiers could identify and arrest only the latter.

3.19   Colonel Wilford either deliberately disobeyed Brigadier MacLellan's order or failed for no good reason to appreciate the clear limits on what he had been authorised to do. He was disturbed by the delay in responding to his request to mount an arrest operation and had concluded that, by reason of the delay, the only way to effect a significant number of arrests was to deploy Support Company in vehicles into the Bogside. He did not inform Brigade of this conclusion. Had he done so, Brigadier MacLellan might well have called off the arrest operation altogether, on the grounds that this deployment would not have provided sufficient separation between rioters and civil rights marchers.

3.20   Colonel Wilford did not pass on to Major Loden (the Commander of Support Company) the Brigadier's injunction on chasing people down Rossville Street, nor did he impose any limits on how far the soldiers of Support Company should go. Colonel Wilford's evidence was that it was not necessary to do either of these things, as he understood the injunction as prohibiting his soldiers from chasing rioters down to Free Derry Corner or beyond and because his soldiers already knew that they should not go further than about 200 or 250 yards from their starting point. Colonel Wilford should have understood that he was being ordered not to chase rioters any distance down Rossville Street.

3.21   The vehicles of Support Company went through Barrier 12. The two leading vehicles, which were Armoured Personnel Carriers (APCs), held soldiers of Mortar Platoon. The first of these vehicles (which carried the Commander of Mortar Platoon, Lieutenant N, and other soldiers) went along Rossville Street and then turned left onto an area of waste ground called the Eden Place waste ground, where the soldiers disembarked. Beyond the waste ground were three high blocks of flats known as the Rossville Flats. In the area partly surrounded by these blocks there was a car park. The second vehicle (under the command of Sergeant O, the Platoon Sergeant of Mortar Platoon) went further along Rossville Street than the first vehicle, stopped briefly on that street where some of the soldiers disembarked, and then turned left and stopped in the entrance to the car park of the Rossville Flats, where the remaining soldiers disembarked. This was about 230 yards from Barrier 12. We set out below a map showing the route these vehicles took and photographs showing the positions they reached, which were in that part of the "no go" area of the city called the Bogside.

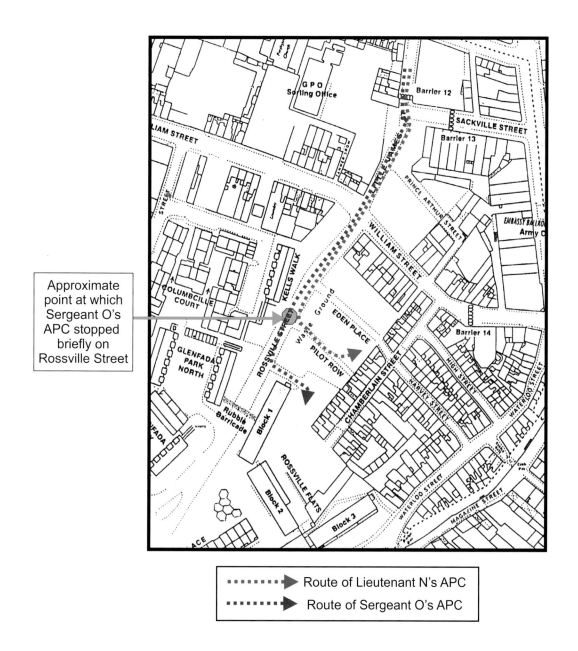

Approximate point at which Sergeant O's APC stopped briefly on Rossville Street

········▶ Route of Lieutenant N's APC
········▶ Route of Sergeant O's APC

Lieutenant N's APC

Rossville Street

Sergeant O's APC

Block 1 of the Rossville Flats

3.22   Many civilians were in the area of the Eden Place waste ground and the car park of the Rossville Flats when the vehicles of Support Company drove into the Bogside. On seeing the Army vehicles these people started to run away. Shortly before it stopped in the car park of the Rossville Flats the vehicle under the command of Sergeant O struck two people, Alana Burke and Thomas Harkin. This was not done deliberately.

3.23   On disembarking soldiers fired baton rounds and some sought to make arrests. Only six arrests were made in this area as the people there when the vehicles arrived rapidly dispersed.

3.24   After disembarking Lieutenant N went towards an alleyway that led from the Eden Place waste ground into Chamberlain Street, which was a street to the east of the Eden Place waste ground that ran parallel to Rossville Street. The alleyway is shown in the following photograph.

3.25   Shortly after arriving at the entrance to the alleyway, Lieutenant N fired two rounds from his rifle over the heads of people who were in the alleyway or in Chamberlain Street at the end of the alleyway and soon afterwards fired a third round in the same direction. These people had come from the area around Barrier 14 in William Street. Some of them had been attempting to rescue a man who had been arrested by one of the soldiers with Lieutenant N and some were throwing stones and similar missiles at the soldiers.

3.26   The shots fired by Lieutenant N hit buildings, but injured no-one. These were the first rifle shots fired in the area after soldiers had gone into the Bogside. Lieutenant N's evidence was that he believed that his shots were the only way of preventing the crowd from attacking him and the soldiers with him. We do not accept that evidence. In our view Lieutenant N probably fired these shots because he decided that this would be an effective way of frightening the people and moving them on, and not because he considered that they posed such a threat to him or the other soldiers that firing his rifle was the only option open to him. In our view this use of his weapon cannot be justified.

The casualties in the Bogside

3.27   Soon after Lieutenant N had fired his shots up the alleyway, soldiers of Mortar Platoon opened fire with their rifles in the area of the car park of the Rossville Flats. In that car park Jackie Duddy (aged 17) was shot and mortally wounded, while Margaret Deery (aged 38), Michael Bridge (aged 25) and Michael Bradley (aged 22) were wounded, all by Army rifle fire. In addition Pius McCarron (aged about 30) and Patrick McDaid (aged 24) suffered injuries from flying debris caused by Army rifle fire. Patrick Brolly (aged 40) was in one of the Rossville Flats and was probably injured by or as the result of Army rifle fire.

3.28   We set out below a diagram showing where these casualties occurred.

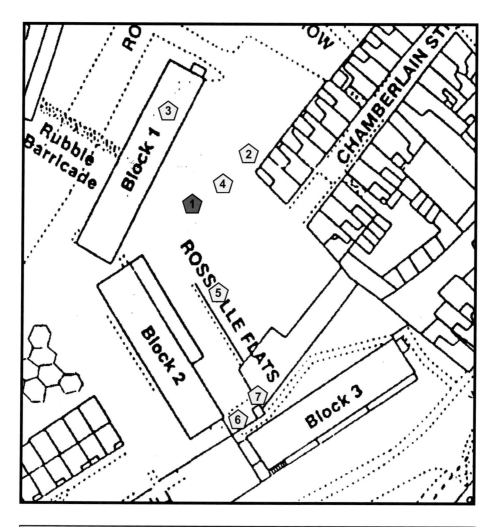

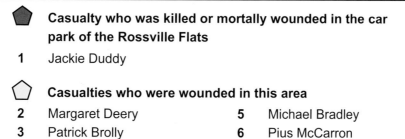

Casualty who was killed or mortally wounded in the car park of the Rossville Flats

1   Jackie Duddy

Casualties who were wounded in this area

2   Margaret Deery   5   Michael Bradley
3   Patrick Brolly   6   Pius McCarron
4   Michael Bridge   7   Patrick McDaid

3.29   Vehicles carrying the Commander of Support Company, Major Loden, and two platoons, Anti-Tank Platoon and Composite Platoon, had followed Mortar Platoon of Support Company into the Bogside. Anti-Tank Platoon was one of the regular platoons of Support Company and was commanded by Lieutenant 119. Composite Platoon was a platoon that was on the day attached to Support Company and was under the command of Captain 200.

3.30   These soldiers disembarked in Rossville Street. Most of the soldiers of Machine Gun
        Platoon remained at this stage in the derelict building on William Street.

3.31   A short time after disembarking, and while events were unfolding in the car park of the
        Rossville Flats, soldiers of Anti-Tank Platoon reached the low walls of a ramp at the
        southern end of a block of flats named Kells Walk, on the western side of Rossville
        Street. Soldiers at that ramp then opened fire with their rifles. One of these shots hit and
        mortally wounded Michael Kelly (aged 17) who was some 80 yards further south behind a
        rubble barricade that had been erected by civilians across Rossville Street before Bloody
        Sunday. We set out below a map showing these positions.

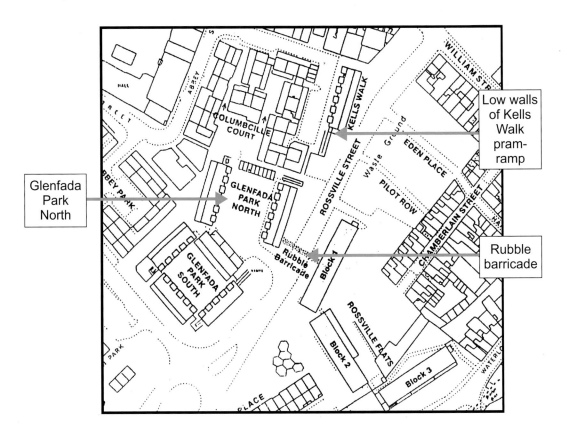

3.32   Soon after civilians had carried Michael Kelly away from the rubble barricade, soldiers in
        Rossville Street fired at and mortally wounded five more people at or in the vicinity of that
        barricade. They were Hugh Gilmour (aged 17), William Nash (aged 19), John Young
        (aged 17), Michael McDaid (aged 20) and Kevin McElhinney (aged 17). In addition
        Alexander Nash (aged 52) was hit and injured by Army gunfire after he had gone to the
        rubble barricade to tend his son William Nash. We set out below a map showing the
        positions where it appears that these casualties occurred. The map also shows where
        Michael Kelly had been shot earlier.

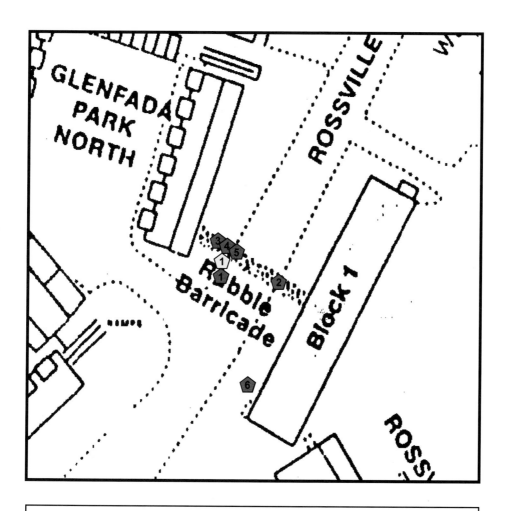

⬠	**Casualties who were killed or mortally wounded in the area of the rubble barricade**
1	Michael Kelly
2	Hugh Gilmour. The precise position at which this casualty was shot is unknown.
3, 4 and 5	Michael McDaid, William Nash and John Young. William Nash was in the middle of the three but the precise position of these casualties at the rubble barricade is not known.
6	Kevin McElhinney
⬠	**Casualty who was wounded in this area**
1	Alexander Nash

3.33   After this firing had begun, soldiers of Anti-Tank Platoon moved forward from the low walls of the Kells Walk ramp and four of them went into Glenfada Park North, a residential building complex that lay to the west of Rossville Street, which is also shown on this map.

3.34   In Glenfada Park North were a number of civilians, many fleeing and seeking refuge from the soldiers.

3.35   Within a few seconds after arriving, the four soldiers who had gone into Glenfada Park North between them shot and mortally wounded William McKinney (aged 26) and Jim Wray (aged 22); and shot and injured Joe Friel (aged 20), Michael Quinn (aged 17), Joe Mahon (aged 16) and Patrick O'Donnell (aged 41). Jim Wray was shot twice, the second time probably as he lay mortally wounded on the ground. We set out below two diagrams showing the area of Glenfada Park North where these casualties occurred. A civilian, Daniel Gillespie (aged 32), may also have been slightly injured by or as the result of Army rifle fire in Glenfada Park North, but this is far from certain.

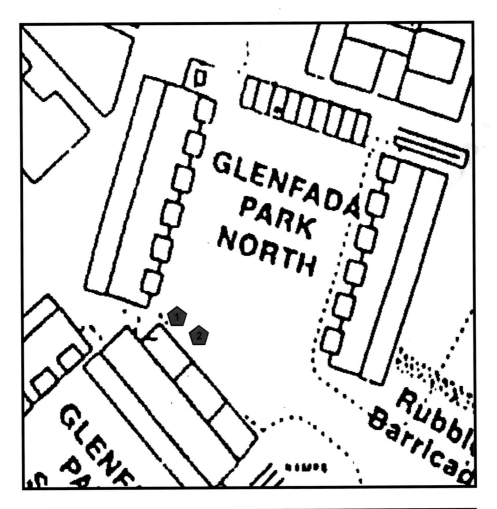

 Casualties who were killed or mortally wounded in Glenfada Park North

1   Jim Wray

2   William McKinney

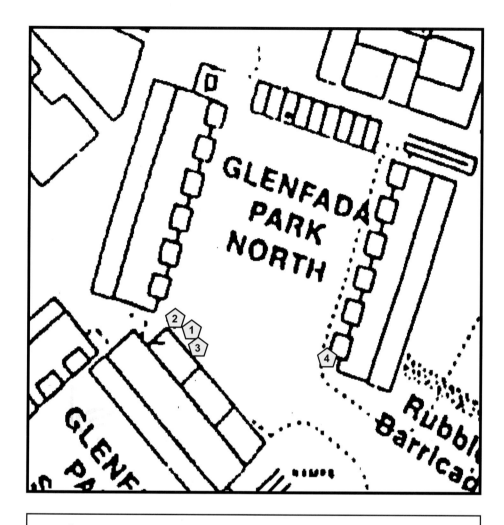

	Casualties who were wounded in Glenfada Park North		
1	Michael Quinn	**3**	Joe Mahon
2	Joe Friel	**4**	Patrick O'Donnell

3.36   One of these soldiers then went from Glenfada Park North to Abbey Park, another residential area which lies to the west of Glenfada Park North, as shown in the following photograph.

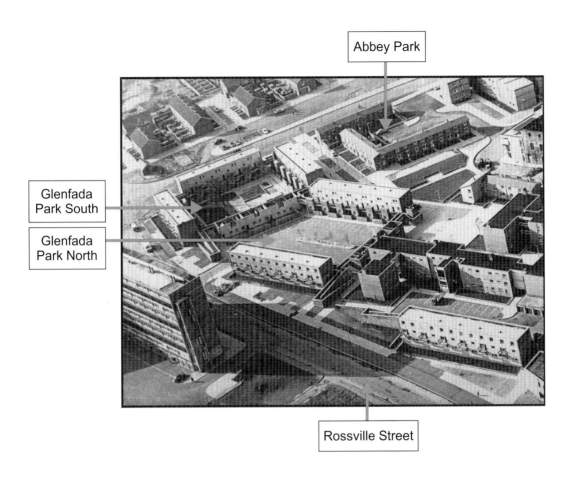

3.37   In Abbey Park this soldier shot and mortally wounded Gerard McKinney (aged 35). His shot passed through this casualty and also mortally wounded Gerald Donaghey (aged 17). We set out below a map showing the area of Abbey Park where these casualties occurred.

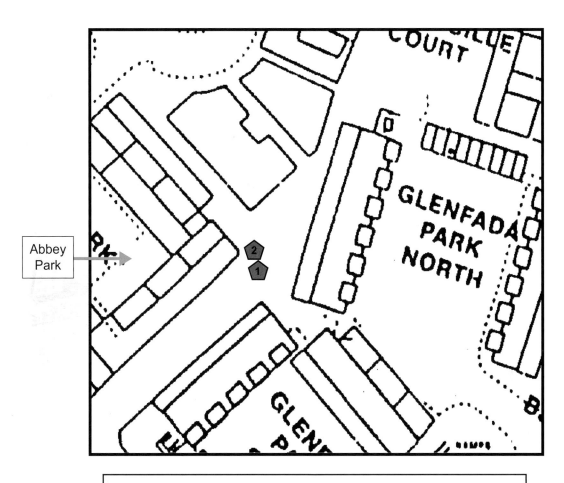

	Casualties who were killed or mortally wounded in Abbey Park
1	Gerard McKinney
2	Gerald Donaghey

3.38   Soon after the shootings in Rossville Street, Glenfada Park North and Abbey Park, some of the soldiers who had been in Glenfada Park North went to its south-east corner, where there was a road entrance to Rossville Street, as shown in the following photograph.

Glenfada Park North

Entrance to Rossville Street

3.39   From this position and again over a very short period of time there was Army gunfire across Rossville Street. This gunfire hit Bernard McGuigan (aged 41) and Patrick Doherty (aged 32), instantly killing the former and mortally wounding the latter. In addition Patrick Campbell (aged 53) and Daniel McGowan (aged 37) were wounded. All these casualties occurred in a pedestrianised area between the Joseph Place flats and the front (southern) side of Block 2 of the Rossville Flats, as shown on the following map.

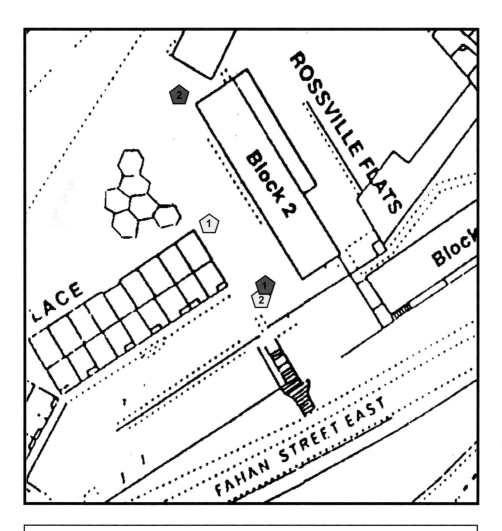

⬠	**Casualties who were killed or mortally wounded between Joseph Place and the Rossville Flats**
1	Patrick Doherty
2	Bernard McGuigan
⬠	**Casualties who were wounded in this area**
1	Patrick Campbell
2	Daniel McGowan

3.40   Although there was later firing by soldiers in Rossville Street, the people shot on the front (southern) side of the Rossville Flats were the last civilians to be shot by the soldiers who had gone into the Bogside.

3.41   Only some ten minutes elapsed between the time soldiers moved in vehicles into the Bogside and the time the last of the civilians was shot.

3.42   There was other firing by the soldiers of Support Company (including soldiers of Composite Platoon) after they had gone into the Bogside, which did not result in death or injury; but which formed an important part of the events of the day and which we consider in this report. In all, soldiers of Support Company fired over 100 rounds after they had gone into the Bogside.

The soldiers who shot the casualties

3.43   We have no doubt that soldiers of Support Company were responsible for all the gunfire casualties that we have described above, using their high velocity self-loading 7.62mm Army rifles, known as SLRs. As will be seen, in some cases we are sure of the identity of the soldier or soldiers concerned, while in other cases our identifications are less certain.

3.44   The first gunfire casualty of the day was Damien Donaghey, who was on a patch of waste ground immediately south of William Street. He was hit in the thigh, either by one of two shots fired by Corporal A or one of three shots fired by Private B, both soldiers of Machine Gun Platoon. The two soldiers fired their shots from the derelict building more or less simultaneously in a single burst of fire. All these shots were aimed and fired at Damien Donaghey.

3.45   Unknown to Corporal A or Private B, fragments from one or more of these shots hit and injured John Johnston, who was on the same patch of waste ground.

3.46   The first casualty of gunfire after soldiers had gone into the Bogside was Jackie Duddy, who was shot and mortally wounded on the western side of the Rossville Flats car park.

3.47   In our view Private R of Mortar Platoon was probably the soldier who aimed at and shot Jackie Duddy. This soldier had disembarked from Sergeant O's APC in Rossville Street, but then ran after this vehicle as it continued into the entrance to the car park of the Rossville Flats, before he fired at Jackie Duddy.

3.48   Soon after Jackie Duddy was shot Lance Corporal V of Mortar Platoon, who had moved towards the car park of the Rossville Flats after disembarking from Lieutenant N's APC, fired his rifle. This shot was probably the one that hit Margaret Deery in the thigh. At the time this casualty was near the southern end of the wall at the back of the gardens of the houses on the western side of Chamberlain Street.

3.49   Michael Bridge was injured after Margaret Deery. He was shot in the thigh when he was a short distance from Sergeant O's vehicle in the car park of the Rossville Flats.

3.50   It is probable that it was Lieutenant N, the Commander of Mortar Platoon, who aimed at and shot Michael Bridge. This officer had moved towards the car park of the Rossville Flats from his APC in the Eden Place waste ground before he fired.

3.51   Michael Bradley was shot when he was on the southern side of the Rossville Flats car park. It is probable that it was Private Q of Mortar Platoon who aimed at and shot Michael Bradley, from a position near to the northern end of Block 1 of the Rossville Flats.

3.52   Patrick McDaid and Pius McCarron were injured by debris sent flying by shots fired as they were attempting to run away from the south-eastern area of the Rossville Flats car park.

3.53   We cannot determine precisely which soldier or soldiers fired these shots beyond saying that it was one or more of Sergeant O, Private R and Private S, all of Mortar Platoon.

3.54   Although he did not aim at Patrick Brolly, Private T of Mortar Platoon was probably responsible for the shot that directly or indirectly injured this casualty, who was in Block 1 of the Rossville Flats. However, we cannot eliminate the possibility that Private S rather than Private T was responsible. Patrick Brolly was injured after Jackie Duddy was shot but before the latter had been carried from the car park.

3.55   We are sure that shortly after he disembarked from his vehicle and while events were unfolding in the car park of the Rossville Flats, Lance Corporal F of Anti-Tank Platoon fired from the low walls of the Kells Walk ramp and mortally injured Michael Kelly, who was behind the rubble barricade in Rossville Street.

3.56   After Michael Kelly had been shot, William Nash, John Young and Michael McDaid were shot and killed at the rubble barricade. We are sure that Corporal P of Mortar Platoon, who had disembarked from Sergeant O's APC in Rossville Street, shot at least one of these casualties and may have been responsible for all three, though Lance Corporal J of Anti-Tank Platoon may have shot one of them and we cannot eliminate the possibility that Corporal E was responsible for another. Corporal P fired from a position in Rossville Street north of the rubble barricade and south of the low walls of the Kells Walk ramp; while Lance Corporal J and Corporal E fired from a position at that ramp.

3.57   We are sure that Private U, a member of Mortar Platoon who had taken up a position at the northern end of Block 1 of the Rossville Flats, fired at and mortally wounded Hugh Gilmour as the latter was running south (ie away from the soldiers) along the Rossville Street side of Block 1 of the Rossville Flats.

3.58   We are sure that either Private L or Private M, members of Composite Platoon who had taken up positions at the low walls of the Kells Walk ramp, shot Kevin McElhinney as he was crawling south from the rubble barricade away from the soldiers. Both probably fired at him on the orders of one or perhaps two nearby non-commissioned officers, Colour Sergeant 002 and Corporal 039.

3.59   It is possible that either Corporal P or Lance Corporal J was responsible for firing at and injuring Alexander Nash. These soldiers were in positions somewhere north of the rubble barricade and south of the low walls of the Kells Walk ramp. However, there is insufficient evidence to make any finding against either of these soldiers on this matter.

3.60   The four soldiers who moved from the low walls of the Kells Walk ramp into Glenfada Park North were Corporal E, Lance Corporal F, Private G and Private H. All were members of Anti-Tank Platoon and all fired their rifles in Glenfada Park North.

3.61   We are sure that these four soldiers were between them responsible for the casualties in Glenfada Park North. It is probable that Corporal E was responsible for the shot that injured Patrick O'Donnell. It is not possible to identify which particular soldiers shot the other casualties. However, we consider it more likely than not that either Lance Corporal F or Private H fired the shot that mortally wounded William McKinney; that one or other of these soldiers was responsible for the shot that wounded Joe Mahon; that either Private G or Private H fired the shot that wounded Michael Quinn; that either Lance Corporal F or Private G fired the shot that wounded Joe Friel; and that either Private G or Private H fired the first shot to hit Jim Wray. Joe Mahon was probably wounded by a shot that had first hit William McKinney. It is not clear whether Joe Friel and Michael Quinn were specifically targeted, or were hit by shots fired indiscriminately at the people who were in the south-west corner of Glenfada Park North. All these shots were fired from the northern side of Glenfada Park North within a very short time of each other. All the casualties were on the southern side of Glenfada Park North, about 40 yards from the soldiers.

3.62   The circumstances in which Daniel Gillespie was injured are so confused that it is not possible to identify the soldier or soldiers who might have been responsible for his injury, which was slight.

3.63   As we have said, Jim Wray was shot twice, the second time probably when he was lying mortally wounded on the ground. It is probable that either Private G or Private H fired this second shot.

3.64   There is no doubt that Private G was the soldier who at a range of only a few yards fired at and mortally wounded Gerard McKinney in Abbey Park. His shot passed through Gerard McKinney's body and also mortally wounded Gerald Donaghey.

3.65   The last gunfire casualties were Bernard McGuigan, Patrick Doherty, Patrick Campbell and Daniel McGowan, all shot in the area to the south of Block 2 of the Rossville Flats within a very short time of each other. We are sure that Lance Corporal F fired at and shot Bernard McGuigan and Patrick Doherty and it is highly probable that he was also responsible for shooting the other two casualties. This soldier fired across Rossville Street from the Rossville Street entranceway into Glenfada Park North.

3.66   We should note at this point that we have considered the possibility that one or more of the casualties might have occurred from soldiers firing by accident, in the sense of discharging their rifles by mistake and without intending to do so. We have found no evidence that suggests to us that this was or might have been the case.

Why the soldiers shot the casualties

3.67   Every soldier serving in Northern Ireland was issued with a card entitled *Instructions by the Director of Operations for Opening Fire in Northern Ireland*. This was known as the Yellow Card, and contained instructions as to when a soldier could open fire.

3.68   The Yellow Card in force on Bloody Sunday contained instructions to the soldiers that they should never use more force than the minimum necessary to enable them to carry out their duties, and should always first try to handle the situation by means other than opening fire. The Yellow Card provided that the soldier should only fire aimed shots and that save in two cases, if a soldier had to open fire, a warning was to be given before doing so. The warning to be given had to include a statement that fire would be opened if the soldier's order was not obeyed.

3.69   The first of the two cases in which a soldier could open fire without warning was when hostile firing was taking place in his area and a warning was impracticable, or when any delay could lead to death or serious injury to people whom it was the soldier's duty to protect or to the soldier himself; and in either of these situations the soldier was only permitted to open fire against a person using a firearm against members of the security forces or people whom it was the soldier's duty to protect; or against a person carrying a firearm if the soldier had reason to think that that person was about to use the firearm for offensive purposes. The Yellow Card defined "firearm" as including a grenade, nail bomb or gelignite-type bomb. The second case in which a soldier could open fire without warning concerned firing at vehicles and has no relevance to the firing on Bloody Sunday.

3.70   None of the casualties shot by soldiers of Support Company was armed with a firearm or (with the probable exception of Gerald Donaghey) a bomb of any description. None was posing any threat of causing death or serious injury. In no case was any warning given before soldiers opened fire.

3.71   It was submitted on behalf of many of the represented soldiers that it was possible that some of the casualties were accidental, in the sense that the soldier concerned fired at someone posing a threat of causing death or serious injury, but missed and hit a bystander instead. It was also submitted that soldiers fired at and killed or injured other people who were posing such a threat, but that the existence of these casualties had been kept secret by those civilians who knew that this had happened, in order to deprive the soldiers of evidence that their firing was justified.

3.72   Apart from the firing by Private T, we have found no substance in either of these submissions.

3.73   As to the first, although John Johnston was hit accidentally from fragments of the shots fired at Damien Donaghey in William Street, Damien Donaghey was not posing a threat of causing death or serious injury. Margaret Deery, who was shot and seriously wounded in the Rossville Flats car park, was probably not the intended target and was hit by accident, but again the soldier concerned was not firing at someone posing a threat of causing death or serious injury. The same is true of the shots that indirectly caused injury to Pius McCarron and Patrick McDaid. In Glenfada Park North, Joe Mahon was hit and wounded by a bullet that was aimed at and probably initially hit William McKinney. In Abbey Park, Gerald Donaghey was hit and mortally wounded by the bullet that had first mortally wounded Gerard McKinney, but neither William McKinney nor Gerard McKinney was posing a threat of causing death or serious injury. Apart from these and Patrick Brolly, all the casualties were either the intended targets of the soldiers or the result of shots fired indiscriminately at people. None of the soldiers admitted missing his target and hitting someone else by mistake.

3.74   As to Patrick Brolly, if Private T was responsible for the shot that injured this casualty, this was one of the two shots that Private T fired at a man who had been throwing down bottles containing acid or a similar corrosive substance from the Rossville Flats.

Such conduct probably did pose a threat of causing serious injury. Private T (if he was responsible) neither intended to hit Patrick Brolly nor fired his rifle indiscriminately at people. If it was Private S who fired and injured Patrick Brolly, he did not aim at this casualty but fired indiscriminately at the Rossville Flats.

3.75 As to the second submission, we are sure that no-one other than the casualties that we have described above was killed or seriously injured by firing by Support Company soldiers. Had there been such casualties, we have no doubt that this would have come to light many years ago. We have found no evidence that suggests to us that there were other less serious casualties of Support Company gunfire.

3.76 Despite the contrary evidence given by soldiers, we have concluded that none of them fired in response to attacks or threatened attacks by nail or petrol bombers. No-one threw or threatened to throw a nail or petrol bomb at the soldiers on Bloody Sunday. There was some firing by republican paramilitaries (though nothing approaching that claimed by some soldiers) which we discuss in detail in this report, but in our view none of this firing provided any justification for the shooting of the civilian casualties. No soldier of Support Company was injured by gunfire on Bloody Sunday. Two suffered slight injuries from acid or a similar corrosive substance thrown down on them in bottles from the Rossville Flats.

3.77 Apart from Private T (who claimed to have fired at someone throwing down acid bombs from the Rossville Flats), all the soldiers who in our view were responsible for the casualties on Bloody Sunday sought to justify their shooting on the grounds that they were sure when they fired that they had targeted and hit someone who was armed with a firearm or a nail or petrol bomb and who was posing or about to pose a threat of causing death or serious injury.

3.78 In other words, all the soldiers (apart from Private T) who were in our view responsible for the casualties insisted that they had shot at gunmen or bombers, which they had not, and (with the possible exception of Lance Corporal F's belated admission with regard to Michael Kelly) did not accept that they had shot the known casualties, which they had. To our minds it inevitably followed that this materially undermined the credibility of the accounts given by the soldiers who fired.

3.79 As we have said, none of the casualties was posing a threat of causing death or serious injury, or indeed was doing anything else that could on any view justify their shooting. However, the question remains as to whether when they fired, the soldiers nevertheless mistakenly believed that they were justified in doing so.

3.80   We appreciate that soldiers on internal security duties, facing a situation in which they or their colleagues may at any moment come under lethal attack, have little time to decide whether they have identified a person posing a threat of causing death or serious injury; and may have to make that decision in a state of tension or fear. It is a well-known phenomenon that, particularly when under stress or when events are moving fast, people often erroneously come to believe that they are or might be hearing or seeing what they were expecting to hear or see. We have borne this in mind when assessing the state of mind of the soldiers responsible for the casualties.

3.81   It is also possible that in the sort of circumstances outlined in the previous paragraph, a soldier might fire in fear or panic, without giving proper thought to whether his target was posing a threat of causing death or serious injury.

3.82   In the course of the report we have considered in detail the accounts of the soldiers whose firing caused the casualties, in the light of much other evidence. We have concluded, for the reasons we give, that apart from Private T many of these soldiers have knowingly put forward false accounts in order to seek to justify their firing. However, we have also borne in mind that the fact that a soldier afterwards lied about what had happened does not necessarily entail that he fired without believing that he had identified a person posing a threat of causing death or serious injury, since it is possible that he was at the time convinced that he was justified in firing, but later invented details in an attempt to bolster his account and make it more credible to others. We have borne this possibility in mind when seeking to decide whether or not each of the soldiers of Support Company who fired and whose shots killed or injured civilians believed, when he did so, that he was justified in firing.

3.83   With these considerations in mind, we turn to consider the individual soldiers concerned. In accordance with our ruling of 11th October 2004,[1] we express where appropriate the degree of confidence or certainty with which we reach our conclusions.

    1 A2.41

3.84   As noted above, the first casualties of Army gunfire on the day were in William Street, some minutes before soldiers went into the Bogside.

3.85   The soldiers concerned in this incident, Corporal A and Private B, unlike those who later went into the Bogside, were not in an open area, but in a derelict building on William Street. At the same time, they were members of a platoon that had been sent to a position isolated from other soldiers, close to the rioting in William Street and adjacent to the

Bogside, the latter being part of the "no go" area of the city and known to be dangerous for the security forces. They accordingly perceived themselves to be in a dangerous situation in which at any time they might be targeted by republican paramilitaries with lethal weapons. If not frightened, they would have been highly apprehensive.

3.86   The evidence of Corporal A and Private B was that the person they shot was about to throw a nail bomb in their direction. This was not the case, though Damien Donaghey had previously been throwing stones at the soldiers and might have been about to do so again. It was submitted on behalf of Damien Donaghey that these soldiers fired without any belief that they had identified someone posing a threat of causing death or serious injury. We concluded that this was not the case and that it was probable that each soldier either mistakenly believed that Damien Donaghey was about to throw a nail bomb or suspected (albeit incorrectly) that he might be about to do so. It is possible that one or both of these soldiers fired in panic or fear, without giving proper thought as to whether his target was posing a threat of causing death or serious injury.

3.87   The next firing by soldiers that resulted in casualties occurred after soldiers had gone into the Bogside. Soldiers of Support Company had been told by officers and believed that this was a particularly dangerous area for the security forces, with any incursion running the risk of meeting attacks by paramilitaries using bombs and firearms. In the minds of some soldiers that belief was reinforced by the shot fired by a member of the Official IRA (OIRA 1) some minutes earlier at soldiers by the Presbyterian church in Great James Street. When they disembarked in the Bogside the soldiers were in an open area where they had never previously been and which was overlooked by the large and high blocks of the Rossville Flats, believed by them to be a place from which republican paramilitaries operated. They were in these circumstances highly alert to the risk of coming under lethal attack from republican paramilitaries either in or near to those flats. Most of the soldiers were armed with rifles to guard against any such attacks and in many cases (in breach of the Yellow Card) had cocked their weapons in order to fire without delay should occasion arise.

3.88   In short, soldiers of Support Company went into what they perceived to be a dangerous area in which they ran the risk of coming under lethal attack at any time. Again, if these soldiers were not frightened, they must at least have been highly apprehensive.

3.89   Since the Eden Place waste ground was an open area, many of the soldiers of Mortar Platoon, and soldiers of the other platoons that had followed Mortar Platoon into the Bogside, must have heard the shots fired by Lieutenant N up the Eden Place alleyway and over the heads of the people there. The effect was to lead at least a number of soldiers to believe either that republican paramilitaries had opened fire or thrown bombs or that a soldier or soldiers were responding to the imminent use of firearms or bombs by paramilitaries; and thus not only to reinforce what they had been told and believed about the likely presence of republican paramilitaries in the area, but also to make them even more ready to respond. If, as we consider was the case, Lieutenant N decided to fire these shots over the heads of the people otherwise than as a last resort to protect himself or other soldiers, he can in our view fairly be criticised, not only for firing, but also for failing to realise the effect that his firing would be likely to have on the other soldiers who had come into the Bogside.

3.90   When shooting breaks out in an urban area, as it then did, it is often difficult or impossible to establish who is firing, from where the firing has come, in what direction it is going, and the type of weapon being used. The same applies to explosions and we have little doubt that the sound of the firing of baton rounds could in some circumstances have been mistaken for the explosion of bombs. In Londonderry these factors were magnified by what was known as "the Derry sound", which was the echoing effect created by the City Walls and adjacent buildings (including the high Rossville Flats) and which could multiply the sound of gunfire and explosions and create false impressions of the direction from which these sounds were coming.

3.91   In circumstances such as we have described, there is a risk that soldiers, mistakenly believing themselves or their colleagues to be under lethal attack, lose their self-control, forget or ignore their training and fire without being satisfied that they have identified a person posing a threat of causing death or serious injury.

3.92   As to the soldiers who went into the Bogside, we have reached the following conclusions.

3.93   As we have said, the first casualty to be shot after the soldiers entered the Bogside was Jackie Duddy, who in our view was probably shot by Private R. According to this soldier's accounts, as he approached Sergeant O's APC he saw and shot a man who was about to throw a nail bomb.

3.94   Jackie Duddy was running away from the soldiers when he was shot. He probably had a stone in his hand at the time. Private R may have thought that Jackie Duddy might have been about to throw a bomb and shot him for this reason, but we are sure that he could not have been sufficiently confident about this to conclude that he was justified in firing. It is possible that Private R fired in a state of fear or panic, giving no proper thought to whether his target was posing a threat of causing death or serious injury.

3.95   The second casualty was Margaret Deery, shot (probably by Lance Corporal V) as she stood with a group of people at or near the southern end of the wall of the gardens of the houses on the western side of Chamberlain Street. Lance Corporal V had approached the car park of the Rossville Flats from Lieutenant N's APC. Lance Corporal V's evidence was that he fired at and hit someone who had thrown or was in the course of throwing a petrol bomb, evidence that we rejected. Margaret Deery was probably not his intended target. Lance Corporal V probably fired in the knowledge that he had not identified someone who was posing a threat of causing death or serious injury. It is possible that he fired in a state of fear or panic, without giving proper thought to whether his target was posing a threat of causing death or serious injury.

3.96   Michael Bridge was shot as he walked towards the soldiers near Sergeant O's vehicle in the car park of the Rossville Flats, shouting at them in protest against the shooting of Jackie Duddy and in his anger inviting the soldiers to shoot him.

3.97   It was probably Lieutenant N who shot Michael Bridge. After firing his rifle up the alleyway leading to Chamberlain Street, Lieutenant N had returned to his vehicle and then moved across the Eden Place waste ground towards the car park of the Rossville Flats. It was at this stage that he fired at and wounded Michael Bridge. His evidence was that he fired at a man he was sure, at the time, was about to throw a nail bomb at his soldiers. In our view Lieutenant N fired, probably either in the mistaken belief that his target was about to throw a nail bomb, but without any adequate grounds for that belief; or in the mistaken belief that his target might have been about to throw a nail bomb, but without being confident that that was so. It is possible that Lieutenant N fired in a state of fear or panic, without giving proper thought to whether his target was posing a threat of causing death or serious injury.

3.98   It was probably Private Q who shot Michael Bradley. This casualty was on the southern side of the Rossville Flats car park and was probably about to throw a stone at the soldiers when he was shot. Private Q falsely maintained that shortly before he fired his shot a nail bomb had been thrown and had exploded in the car park and that he was sure that the person he shot was about to throw another nail bomb, but we are sure that Private Q did not believe when he fired that he had identified a nail bomber. It is possible that he mistakenly thought that Michael Bradley might have been about to throw a bomb, but in our view, even if this was so, he could not have been sufficiently confident about this to conclude that he was justified in firing. It is possible that Private Q fired in a state of fear or panic, giving no proper thought to whether his target was posing a threat of causing death or serious injury.

3.99   One or more of Sergeant O, Private R and Private S fired the shots that indirectly injured Patrick McDaid and Pius McCarron. All these soldiers claimed to have fired at gunmen at ground level, a claim we do not accept. While they did not aim at either Patrick McDaid or Pius McCarron, we are sure that the soldier or soldiers whose shots resulted in these casualties fired without justification and without any or any proper regard to the risk to people in the area.

3.100   Private T was probably responsible for the shot that directly or indirectly injured Patrick Brolly, who was in Block 1 of the Rossville Flats, though it is possible that Private S was responsible. The soldier concerned did not aim at Patrick Brolly. If it was a shot by Private S (who fired 12 shots in the area of the Rossville Flats car park) we are sure that it was fired for no good reason and without any regard to the risk to people in the flats. If it was Private T, it was one of two shots that this soldier fired at a man on a balcony of Block 1 of the Rossville Flats, who had thrown down at the soldiers below a bottle or bottles containing acid or a similar corrosive substance, which had caused minor injuries to Private T and Private R. These shots were fired without a previous warning and thus in our view contravened the instructions given to the soldiers as to when they could open fire, contained in the Yellow Card. Sergeant O had told Private T to shoot if the man sought to throw another bottle. Both he and Private T believed that the person concerned was posing a threat of causing serious injury. The second shot was fired after the man had thrown a further bottle and thus at a time when he was posing no threat to the soldiers. Both shots missed the intended target.

3.101   In Rossville Street, Lance Corporal F fired from the low walls of the Kells Walk ramp and killed Michael Kelly who was behind the rubble barricade on Rossville Street, some 80 yards away. Initially Lance Corporal F said nothing about this shot but later he admitted that he had fired, falsely claiming that this was at a nail bomber. In our view Lance Corporal F did not fire in panic or fear, without giving proper thought to whether he had identified a person posing a threat of causing death or serious injury. We are sure that instead he fired either in the belief that no-one at the rubble barricade was posing a threat of causing death or serious injury, or not caring whether or not anyone at the rubble barricade was posing such a threat.

3.102   As to the further shooting in Rossville Street, which caused the deaths of William Nash, John Young and Michael McDaid, Corporal P claimed that he fired at a man with a pistol; Lance Corporal J claimed that he fired at a nail bomber; and Corporal E claimed that he fired at a man with a pistol in the Rossville Flats. We reject each of these claims as knowingly untrue. We are sure that these soldiers fired either in the belief that no-one in the areas towards which they respectively fired was posing a threat of causing death or serious injury, or not caring whether or not anyone there was posing such a threat. In their cases we consider that they did not fire in a state of fear or panic.

3.103   We take the same view of the shot that we are sure Private U fired at Hugh Gilmour, mortally wounding this casualty as he was running away from the soldiers. We reject as knowingly untrue Private U's account of firing at a man with a handgun.

3.104   As we have explained, either Private L or Private M shot and mortally wounded Kevin McElhinney as he was crawling away from the soldiers. They probably did so on the orders of Colour Sergeant 002 or Corporal 039 or perhaps both these non-commissioned officers.

3.105   These soldiers and officers gave evidence that they had seen two people, one or both with rifles, crawling away from the rubble barricade. They probably believed that they might have identified a gunman or gunmen, but none of them could have been satisfied that they had done so. Their targets were crawling away and not posing an immediate threat of causing death or serious injury. The soldiers' evidence was that they fired, not because the crawling men were posing at that moment an immediate threat of causing death or serious injury, but because they believed that the crawling men would or might use their weapons once they had reached cover, although Private L expressed the view that he was entitled to fire at someone with a weapon, whatever that individual was doing. These shots were not fired in fear or panic. We are of the view that the soldiers concerned probably believed that the crawling men might pose a threat of causing death or serious injury once they had reached cover, though it is possible that Private L did not care whether or not they would pose such a threat.

3.106   We are sure that the soldier who shot and injured Alexander Nash while he was tending his dead or dying son William at the rubble barricade could not have believed that he had or might have identified someone posing a threat of causing death or serious injury.

3.107   We have above identified Corporal E, Lance Corporal F, Private G and Private H as the soldiers who went into Glenfada Park North, between them killing William McKinney and Jim Wray, injuring Joe Mahon, Joe Friel, Michael Quinn and Patrick O'Donnell, and possibly injuring Daniel Gillespie. All claimed that they had identified and shot at people in possession of or seeking to use bombs or firearms.

3.108   In our view none of these soldiers fired in the belief that he had or might have identified a person in possession of or using or about to use bombs or firearms. William McKinney and Jim Wray were both shot in the back and none of the other casualties (with the possible exception of Daniel Gillespie) appears to have been facing the soldiers when shot. We are sure that these soldiers fired either in the belief that no-one in the areas towards which they respectively fired was posing a threat of causing death or serious injury, or not caring whether or not anyone there was posing such a threat. In their cases (with the possible exception of Private H), it is unlikely that they fired in a state of fear or panic.

3.109 All four soldiers denied shooting anyone on the ground. However, Jim Wray was shot for a second time in the back, probably as he lay mortally wounded in the south-western corner of Glenfada Park North. Whichever soldier was responsible for firing the second shot, we are sure that he must have known that there was no possible justification for shooting Jim Wray as he lay on the ground.

3.110 Private G shot Gerard McKinney in Abbey Park. As we have already noted, his shot passed through this casualty and mortally wounded Gerald Donaghey. Private G may not have been aware that his shot had had this additional effect. Private G falsely denied that he had fired in Abbey Park. He did not fire in fear or panic and we are sure that he must have fired knowing that Gerard McKinney was not posing a threat of causing death or serious injury.

3.111 Gerald Donaghey was taken by car to the Regimental Aid Post of 1st Battalion, The Royal Anglian Regiment, which was at the western end of Craigavon Bridge, which spans the River Foyle. There four nail bombs were found in his pockets. The question arose as to whether the nail bombs were in his pockets when he was shot, or had been planted on him later by the security forces. We have considered the substantial amount of evidence relating to this question and have concluded, for reasons that we give, that the nail bombs were probably on Gerald Donaghey when he was shot. However, we are sure that Gerald Donaghey was not preparing or attempting to throw a nail bomb when he was shot; and we are equally sure that he was not shot because of his possession of nail bombs. He was shot while trying to escape from the soldiers.

3.112 As we have said, the last gunfire casualties were Bernard McGuigan, Patrick Doherty, Patrick Campbell and Daniel McGowan, all shot in the area to the south of Block 2 of the Rossville Flats within a very short time of each other. Bernard McGuigan was shot in the head and killed instantly as he was waving a piece of cloth and moving out from the cover afforded by the southern end wall of Block 1 of the Rossville Flats. Further to the east Patrick Doherty was shot in the buttock and mortally wounded as he was attempting to crawl to safety across the area that lay on the southern side of Block 2 of the Rossville

Flats. Patrick Campbell was shot in the back and injured as he ran away from the southern end of Block 1 of the Rossville Flats along the southern side of Block 2. Daniel McGowan was shot and injured in the leg when he was in about the same area as where Patrick Doherty was shot.

3.113   We have no doubt that Lance Corporal F shot Patrick Doherty and Bernard McGuigan, and it is highly probable that he also shot Patrick Campbell and Daniel McGowan. In 1972 Lance Corporal F initially said nothing about firing along the pedestrianised area on the southern side of Block 2 of the Rossville Flats, but later admitted that he had done so. No other soldier claimed or admitted to firing into this area. Lance Corporal F's claim that he had fired at a man who had (or, in one account, was firing) a pistol was to his knowledge false. Lance Corporal F did not fire in a state of fear or panic. We are sure that he fired either in the belief that no-one in the area into which he fired was posing a threat of causing death or serious injury, or not caring whether or not anyone there was posing such a threat.

Other firing by soldiers on Bloody Sunday

3.114   Soldiers of Support Company fired in all over 100 rifle rounds on Bloody Sunday after they had gone into the Bogside. In this report we describe in detail not only the circumstances in which soldiers fired and killed or injured civilians, but also the circumstances in which the other shooting occurred. As to the latter, with the probable exception of shots fired by Sergeant O at what he described as a gunman on a balcony of Block 3 of the Rossville Flats, we found no instances where it appeared to us that soldiers either were or might have been justified in firing. In many cases the soldiers concerned fired either in the belief that no-one in the areas into which they fired was posing a threat of causing death or serious injury, or not caring whether or not anyone there was posing such a threat; while in other cases we consider that when the soldiers fired they may have mistakenly suspected, without being satisfied, that they might have identified someone posing a threat of causing death or serious injury.

3.115   Apart from the firing by soldiers of Support Company, there was no other firing by members of 1 PARA on Bloody Sunday. In particular, there was no firing by members of C Company, who had also gone into the Bogside (on foot through Barrier 14) soon after Support Company had gone through Barrier 12.

3.116   There were other incidents of Army firing on Bloody Sunday, by members of other Army units. This firing was in response to republican paramilitary firing that was directed at soldiers, but not at those who had gone into the Bogside. We consider these incidents in detail in this report. In one of these incidents (some 600 yards from the area where the civilians were killed and injured by soldiers of Support Company) a soldier (in our view justifiably) shot at and injured an armed member of the Official IRA, "Red" Mickey Doherty, who had immediately before fired at soldiers.

3.117   At one stage it was suggested that a soldier or soldiers stationed on the City Walls above the area into which Support Company of 1 PARA deployed might have been responsible for some of the civilian casualties at the rubble barricade in Rossville Street. We considered this possibility but are sure, for the reasons we give in the report, that this was not the case; and by the end of the Inquiry no-one taking part in the Inquiry suggested otherwise.

3.118   As will be seen from this report, as part of our investigation we examined in detail the organisation of the Provisional and Official IRA and the activities of members of those organisations on the day, since it was submitted on behalf of soldiers that, in effect, these activities justified the soldiers opening fire. With the exception of Gerald Donaghey, who was a member of the Provisional IRA's youth wing, the Fianna, none of those killed or wounded by soldiers of Support Company belonged to either the Provisional or the Official IRA.

3.119   In the course of investigating the activities of the Provisional and Official IRA on the day, we considered at some length allegations that Martin McGuinness, at that time the Adjutant of the Derry Brigade or Command of the Provisional IRA, had engaged in paramilitary activity during the day. In the end we were left in some doubt as to his movements on the day. Before the soldiers of Support Company went into the Bogside he was probably armed with a Thompson sub-machine gun, and though it is possible that he fired this weapon, there is insufficient evidence to make any finding on this, save that we are sure that he did not engage in any activity that provided any of the soldiers with any justification for opening fire.

The arrest of civilians

3.120   Soldiers of Support Company, 1 PARA arrested a number of civilians on Bloody Sunday. Only six were arrested in the area of Rossville Street or in the Eden Place waste ground where the soldiers had initially deployed, most of the others being arrested either in a house in Chamberlain Street or where they had taken shelter behind a wall at the south-eastern corner of Glenfada Park North. In this report, we have examined the circumstances of these arrests and what happened to those who were arrested, not only because they formed an important part of the events of the day, but because the way in which some were treated provided an indication of the attitude that some soldiers of 1 PARA adopted towards the people they encountered on Bloody Sunday. There were a number of incidents in which soldiers gave knowingly false accounts of the circumstances in which arrests were made. In the end no proceedings were pursued against any of those who had been arrested.

Chapter 4: The question of responsibility for the deaths and injuries on Bloody Sunday

Contents

4.1   The immediate responsibility for the deaths and injuries on Bloody Sunday lies with those members of Support Company whose unjustifiable firing was the cause of those deaths and injuries. The question remains, however, as to whether others also bear direct or indirect responsibility for what happened.

The United Kingdom and Northern Ireland Governments and the Army

4.2   During the course of the Inquiry, allegations were made by some of those representing the families of those who died on Bloody Sunday and those wounded, that the politicians in both the United Kingdom and Northern Ireland Governments, as well as the military authorities, had planned not simply to stop the civil rights march and to mount an arrest operation against rioters as set out in the orders for Operation Forecast (the operation to contain the march and deal with any rioting), but rather to use 1 PARA for the purpose of carrying out some action, which they knew would involve the deliberate use of unwarranted lethal force or which they sanctioned with reckless disregard as to whether such force was used. On this basis it was submitted that the civil and military authorities bore responsibility for the deaths and injuries on Bloody Sunday.

4.3   These allegations were based on one of two propositions, either that what happened on Bloody Sunday was intended and planned by the authorities, or that it was foreseen by the authorities as likely to happen. We are of the view that neither of these propositions can be sustained.

4.4   In order to consider these allegations we looked in detail at what the authorities were planning and doing in the weeks and months preceding Bloody Sunday; as well as what happened on Bloody Sunday before soldiers were sent into the Bogside. We found no evidence to substantiate these allegations. So far as the United Kingdom Government was concerned, what the evidence did establish was that in the months before Bloody Sunday, genuine and serious attempts were being made at the highest level to work towards a peaceful political settlement in Northern Ireland. Any action involving the use or likely use of unwarranted lethal force against nationalists on the occasion of the march (or otherwise) would have been entirely counterproductive to the plans for a peaceful settlement; and was neither contemplated nor foreseen by the United Kingdom Government. So far as the Northern Ireland Government was concerned, although it had been pressing the United Kingdom Government and the Army to step up their efforts to counter republican paramilitaries and to deal with banned marches, we found no evidence that suggested to us that it advocated the use of unwarranted lethal force or was indifferent to its use on the occasion of the march.

4.5   It was also submitted that in dealing with the security situation in Northern Ireland generally, the authorities (the United Kingdom and Northern Ireland Governments and the Army) tolerated if not encouraged the use of unjustified lethal force; and that this was the cause or a contributory cause of what happened on Bloody Sunday. We found no evidence of such toleration or encouragement.

4.6   There was a further submission to the effect that it was critical to an understanding of why lethal force was used by the Army against unarmed civilians on Bloody Sunday, to appreciate that by this time the role of the police in security matters had been eroded and that the Army had illegally taken control over the policing of security situations from the police. Though by the period in question the situation was such that the RUC had neither the manpower nor the resources to deal effectively with all security issues and was in many cases dependent upon the military, we do not accept that the Army had illegally taken over control of security from the police. The Army and the police worked together in deciding how to deal with matters of security.

4.7 As to the actions of the soldiers themselves, it was submitted that those who fired did so because of a "*culture*" that had grown up among soldiers at the time in Northern Ireland, to the effect that they could fire with impunity, secure in the knowledge that the arrangements then in force (arrangements later criticised by the Lord Chief Justice of Northern Ireland) meant that their actions would not be investigated by the RUC, but by the Royal Military Police (the Army's own police force), who would be sympathetic to the soldiers and who would not conduct a proper investigation. In support of this submission it was alleged that before Bloody Sunday there were many previous unjustified shooting incidents by soldiers in Northern Ireland. As we pointed out in the course of the Inquiry, it was simply not possible to take this submission of an established "*culture*" forward, for this could only be done by examining in the same detail as Bloody Sunday the circumstances of each of those incidents, in order to decide, among other things, whether or not they involved unjustified firing by soldiers. In our view this would have been a wholly impracticable course for us to take, adding immeasurably to what was already a very long and complex inquiry. In these circumstances, we are not in a position to express a view either as to whether or not such a culture existed among soldiers before Bloody Sunday or, if it did, whether it had any influence on those who fired unjustifiably on that day.

Major General Ford

4.8 In the light of the situation that obtained in Londonderry in early 1972 (which we discuss in detail in this report), we do not criticise General Ford for deciding to deploy soldiers to arrest rioters, though in our view his decision to use 1 PARA as the arrest force is open to criticism, on the ground that 1 PARA was a force with a reputation for using excessive physical violence, which thus ran the risk of exacerbating the tensions between the Army and nationalists in Londonderry. However, there is to our minds a significant difference between the risk of soldiers using excessive physical violence when dispersing crowds or trying to arrest rioters and the risk that they would use lethal weapons without justification. We have concluded that General Ford had no reason to believe and did not believe that the risk of soldiers of 1 PARA firing unjustifiably during the course of an arrest operation was such that it was inappropriate for that reason for him to use them for such an operation.

4.9   General Ford denied, both to the Widgery Inquiry and to the present Inquiry, that the Army plan for 30th January 1972 was to cause a confrontation with the IRA, Official, Provisional or both. We accept his denial. We are sure that there was no such plan.

4.10   As to General Ford's memorandum, where he suggested shooting selected ringleaders of rioters after warning, we are surprised that an officer of his seniority should seriously consider that this was something that could be done, notwithstanding that he acknowledged that to take this course would require authorisation from above. We are sure, for the reasons given in the report, that this idea was not adopted and that the shootings on Bloody Sunday were not the result of any plan to shoot selected ringleaders. In the event General Ford decided to use an additional battalion (1 PARA) as the means of seeking to deal with rioters. We found no evidence to suggest that the use of lethal force against unarmed rioters, who were not posing a threat of causing death or serious injury, was contemplated by General Ford or those senior to him as a possible means of dealing with any rioting that might accompany the then forthcoming civil rights march.

4.11   General Ford did not himself play any role in ordering the arrest operation to be launched or in determining the form either in which Brigade ordered it or which it actually took. He did not seek to interfere with or to influence what happened to any significant extent and was right not to do so, since the decision whether to launch an arrest operation and the form that it was to take were matters for Brigadier MacLellan.

4.12   General Ford was responsible for deciding that in the likely event of rioting, Brigade should employ 1 PARA as an arrest force on 30th January 1972. But he neither knew nor had reason to know at any stage that his decision would or was likely to result in soldiers firing unjustifiably on that day.

Brigadier MacLellan

4.13   As we have noted above, the power to order an arrest operation did not rest with General Ford, but with Brigadier MacLellan. We do not criticise Brigadier MacLellan for giving such an order. As we have pointed out, he did not do so until he was reasonably satisfied that there was sufficient separation between rioters and peaceful marchers to sanction the limited arrest operation that had been initially suggested by Colonel Wilford. Had Colonel Wilford informed him that the situation had changed and that as the commander of the arrest force he now considered that it was necessary to order an additional company to go in vehicles along Rossville Street in order to arrest rioters, Brigadier MacLellan might well have abandoned the arrest operation altogether, on the ground that such an operation would not allow sufficient separation between marchers and rioters. Brigadier MacLellan had no reason to believe and did not believe that the limited arrest operation he ordered ran the risk of deaths or injuries from unjustifiable firing by soldiers.

4.14   We should add at this point that in our view Brigadier MacLellan cannot fairly be criticised either for not imposing additional restrictions on when soldiers could open fire, over and above those in the Yellow Card; or for failing to order soldiers engaged in an arrest operation to disengage rather than respond if they were or believed that they were under attack from republican paramilitaries, so as to minimise the risk that innocent civilians would be killed or injured. In his case suggestions to the contrary incorrectly assume that he bears responsibility for sending soldiers into the Bogside. The arrest operation Brigadier MacLellan ordered was limited in scope and would not have involved soldiers going into the Bogside to any or any significant extent; and in our view the risk to civilians from such an operation did not call for any such special restrictions or special orders. We have concluded that Brigadier MacLellan does not bear any responsibility for the deaths and injuries from the unjustifiable firing by soldiers on Bloody Sunday.

Lieutenant Colonel Wilford

4.15   What did happen was not what Colonel Wilford had initially suggested and Brigadier MacLellan had then ordered. Colonel Wilford should have ordered his soldiers to stay in and around William Street and the northern end of Rossville Street. Instead, he sent them into the Bogside, where they chased people down Rossville Street, into the car park of the Rossville Flats, into Glenfada Park North and as far as Abbey Park.

4.16   In our view Colonel Wilford decided to send Support Company into the Bogside because at the time he gave the order he had concluded (without informing Brigadier MacLellan) that there was now no prospect of making any or any significant arrests in the area he had originally suggested, as the rioting was dying down and people were moving away. In addition it appears to us that he wanted to demonstrate that the way to deal with rioters in Londonderry was not for soldiers to shelter behind barricades like (as he put it) "*Aunt Sallies*" while being stoned, as he perceived the local troops had been doing, but instead to go aggressively after rioters, as he and his soldiers had been doing in Belfast.

4.17   What Colonel Wilford failed to appreciate, or regarded as of little consequence, was that his soldiers, who had not been in a position to observe the rioting that had been going on at the Army barriers, would almost certainly be unable to identify anyone as a rioter, save where, when they arrived, they were met by people who were rioting at that time.

4.18   Colonel Wilford failed to inform Brigade that in his view the situation had changed and that the only prospect of making any arrests was to send his soldiers in vehicles into the Bogside. He then failed to obey the order that Brigadier MacLellan gave, which prohibited any such movement. He thus created a situation in which soldiers chased people down Rossville Street and beyond, in circumstances where it was not possible to distinguish between those who had merely been marching and those who had been rioting. His failure to comply with his orders, instead setting in train the very thing his Brigadier had prohibited him from doing, cannot be justified.

4.19   In our view Colonel Wilford can also be criticised on another ground. He sent his soldiers into an area which he regarded as dangerous and which he had told his soldiers was dangerous; an area which his soldiers did not know and where they might come under lethal attack from republican paramilitaries, who dominated that part of the city. He knew that his soldiers would accordingly be very much on their guard, ready to respond instantly with gunfire at identified targets, as they were trained to respond, if they did come under such attack. He knew that his soldiers would not withdraw if they came under lethal attack but were trained not just to take cover, but instead to move forward and, as he himself put it, seek out the "*enemy*".

4.20   In these circumstances, on his own estimation of the danger of lethal attacks by republican paramilitaries, Colonel Wilford must have appreciated that there was a significant risk that sending his soldiers into the Bogside on an arrest operation could lead to an armed engagement with republican paramilitaries. He should have appreciated that if this did happen, then there was also, in view of the numbers of people around, a significant risk that people other than soldiers' justifiable targets would be killed or injured, albeit by accident, from Army gunfire. To our minds this was another reason why Colonel Wilford should not have launched an incursion into the Bogside.

4.21   The fact that what in the event happened on Bloody Sunday when the soldiers entered the Bogside was not a justifiable response to a lethal attack by republican paramilitaries, but instead soldiers opening fire unjustifiably, cannot provide an answer to this criticism, which is based not on what happened, but what at the time Colonel Wilford thought might happen.

4.22   We have found nothing that suggests to us that Colonel Wilford can be blamed for the incident in which soldiers fired from the derelict building in William Street and injured Damien Donaghey and John Johnston. However, the question remains as to whether he realised, or should have realised, that the risk of unjustifiable firing by soldiers if he sent them into the Bogside was such that for this reason he should not have ordered them to go in.

4.23   As one of the officers (given the cipher Captain 128), who was a member of 2nd Battalion, The Royal Green Jackets and was present on the day, told us, when a soldier hears shots and believes that he is under fire, his automatic reaction is to fire himself, which is a difficult reaction to stop; and when firing breaks out in a tense situation it can spread very quickly and is very difficult to control. It could thus be said that Colonel Wilford should have appreciated that by sending soldiers into an unfamiliar area, which they had been told was and which they perceived to be a dangerous area, there was a risk that they might mistakenly believe that they had come under attack from republican paramilitaries and in that belief open fire without being satisfied that they had identified people who were posing a threat of causing death or serious injury; and that because of that risk, he should not have sent soldiers into the Bogside. In the end, however, we consider that on this specific ground Colonel Wilford cannot fairly be criticised for giving the orders he did. We take the view that Colonel Wilford cannot be blamed for failing to foresee that the risk of his soldiers firing unjustifiably was such that he should not have given the orders he did.

4.24   In summary, therefore, in our view Colonel Wilford should not have sent soldiers of Support Company into the Bogside for the following reasons:

- because in doing so he disobeyed the orders given by Brigadier MacLellan;

- because his soldiers, whose job was to arrest rioters, would have no or virtually no means of identifying those who had been rioting from those who had simply been taking part in the civil rights march; and

- because he should not have sent his soldiers into an unfamiliar area which he and they regarded as a dangerous area, where the soldiers might come under attack from republican paramilitaries, in circumstances where the soldiers' response would run a significant risk that people other than those engaging the soldiers with lethal force would be killed or injured by Army gunfire.

4.25   There remains the suggestion that Colonel Wilford's soldiers should have been instructed that in order to minimise the risk to innocent people, if on going into the Bogside they came under attack from paramilitaries, or believed that this had happened, they should disengage and withdraw rather than return fire. In our view this is a hypothetical question, since for the first two of the reasons we have given above Colonel Wilford should not have sent soldiers into the Bogside, with or without special instructions.

Major Loden

4.26   Those representing the families of the deceased and the wounded criticised Major Loden, the Commander of Support Company, on the ground that he failed to exercise any proper control over his soldiers or their firing.

4.27   In our view, events moved so fast after the soldiers had disembarked in the Bogside that Major Loden had no idea what was actually going on; he assumed that his soldiers had come under attack from republican paramilitaries and were responding. It could be said that another officer in Major Loden's position might have appreciated earlier that, in view of the amount of Army gunfire, something seemed to be going seriously wrong; republican paramilitaries were not known to take on troops in force, but usually sniped at individuals from positions of cover. In consequence such an officer might have made greater efforts to control the situation.

4.28   Major Loden was surprised by the amount of firing. However, he did not initially appreciate that something was wrong and did not order a ceasefire or give any other instructions to his soldiers until after all the casualties had been sustained. We consider that it was not unreasonable for him initially to believe, as he did, that his soldiers, by going into an area dominated by paramilitaries, had for once encountered paramilitary resistance in strength, to which they were responding. We accept his evidence that in this belief, it was not for him to control or stop his soldiers' firing, but to leave this to the platoon and section commanders. We also accept, for the reasons he gave, that he could not see the targets that his soldiers were engaging and thus could not tell whether or not the firing was unjustified.

4.29   In our view, at the time the casualties were being sustained, Major Loden neither realised nor should have realised that his soldiers were or might be firing at people who were not posing or about to pose a threat of causing death or serious injury. However, we consider that at the time when he did tell his soldiers not to fire back unless they had identified positive targets, he probably did realise that the firing that was taking place then was, or might be, unjustified. By this stage all the casualties had been sustained and there had been a pause in the firing.

Lieutenant N

4.30   Lieutenant N, the Commander of Mortar Platoon, failed to appreciate, as he should have done, that firing unjustified shots over the heads of people in the alleyway leading into Chamberlain Street was likely to lead other soldiers mistakenly to believe, as some probably did, that Support Company was at that time coming under attack or the threat of attack from republican paramilitaries. As we have said, he was probably responsible for shooting Michael Bridge. However, we take the view that there was in the circumstances (and bearing particularly in mind the speed of events) nothing (apart from refraining from firing his unjustified shots over the heads of people) that he could or should have done to avert the shooting by other members of his platoon. We are not persuaded that he should have realised at the time that his soldiers were firing unjustifiably.

Lieutenant 119

4.31   Lieutenant 119 was the Commander of Anti-Tank Platoon. We criticise this officer for allowing four members of his platoon to go into Glenfada Park North, out of his sight and control. Before this happened he appears to have been labouring under the mistaken belief that his soldiers at the low walls of the Kells Walk ramp were responding to paramilitary attacks. We are not persuaded that he should have realised that these soldiers were firing unjustifiably.

Captain 200 and Sergeant INQ 441

4.32   Captain 200 was the Commander of Composite Platoon. There is nothing to suggest that he, or Sergeant INQ 441, the Commander of Machine Gun Platoon, was responsible for any of the unjustifiable firing by his soldiers.

The Northern Ireland Civil Rights Association

4.33   In our view the organisers of the civil rights march bear no responsibility for the deaths and injuries on Bloody Sunday. Although those who organised the march must have realised that there was probably going to be trouble from rioters, they had no reason to believe and did not believe that this was likely to result in death or injury from unjustified firing by soldiers.

Chapter 5: The overall assessment

5.1   The early firing in William Street resulted in two wounded casualties, neither of whom was doing anything that justified either of them being shot. It is possible that the soldiers concerned mistakenly believed that they had identified someone posing a threat of causing death or serious injury. Equally, each of those soldiers may have fired, not believing that his target was posing a threat of causing death or serious injury, but only suspecting that this might have been the case.

5.2   The soldiers of Support Company who went into the Bogside did so as the result of an order by Colonel Wilford, which should not have been given and which was contrary to the orders that he had received from Brigadier MacLellan.

5.3   With the exception of Private T and with the probable exception of shots Sergeant O said that he fired at someone on a balcony of Block 3 of the Rossville Flats and which, (despite his assertion to the contrary) did not hit anyone, none of the firing by the soldiers of Support Company was aimed at people posing a threat of causing death or serious injury.

5.4   We have concluded that the explanation for such firing by Support Company soldiers after they had gone into the Bogside was in most cases probably the mistaken belief among them that republican paramilitaries were responding in force to their arrival in the Bogside. This belief was initiated by the first shots fired by Lieutenant N and reinforced by the further shots that followed soon after. In this belief soldiers reacted by losing their self-control and firing themselves, forgetting or ignoring their instructions and training and failing to satisfy themselves that they had identified targets posing a threat of causing death or serious injury. In the case of those soldiers who fired in either the knowledge or belief that no-one in the areas into which they fired was posing a threat of causing death or serious injury, or not caring whether or not anyone there was posing such a threat, it is at least possible that they did so in the indefensible belief that all the civilians they fired at were probably either members of the Provisional or Official IRA or were supporters of one or other of these paramilitary organisations; and so deserved to be shot notwithstanding that they were not armed or posing any threat of causing death or serious injury. Our overall conclusion is that there was a serious and widespread loss of fire discipline among the soldiers of Support Company.

5.5　　The firing by soldiers of 1 PARA on Bloody Sunday caused the deaths of 13 people and injury to a similar number, none of whom was posing a threat of causing death or serious injury. What happened on Bloody Sunday strengthened the Provisional IRA, increased nationalist resentment and hostility towards the Army and exacerbated the violent conflict of the years that followed. Bloody Sunday was a tragedy for the bereaved and the wounded, and a catastrophe for the people of Northern Ireland.